DISCARD

S0-BCL-768

the true book of

TRAVEL

BY WATER

140576

John Hornby

Illustrated by
VIRGINIA SMITH

DISCARD

RETURN TO
CAMPBELL UNION SCHOOL
DISTRICT LIBRARY

 CHILDRENS PRESS, CHICAGO

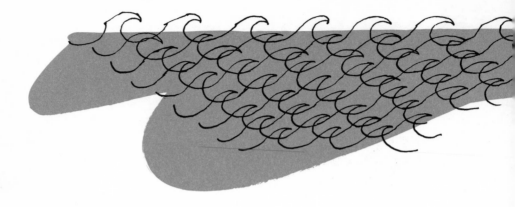

To Alice Winifred Hornby

Library of Congress Catalog Card Number: 69-14682

Copyright © in Great Britain, 1968, John Hornby and Virginia Smith

This edition published, 1969, by Childrens Press,
through the courtesy of Oliver & Boyd, Ltd., London
Printed in the U.S.A.

140576

There are many things which will float without sinking under the weight of a man.

Men have made full use of them to travel by water in search of food or new land, or simply to see how far they could go.

There is a great deal of water to travel over in the world.

For use on rivers and lakes and sheltered water only the smallest and simplest of craft were needed — bundles of reeds, small rafts, simple boats and canoes.

Rafts are easily made of reeds, logs or tree trunks, but men have traveled amazing distances on them.

The peoples of the Pacific islands
probably drifted thousands of miles
across the Pacific, as the raft
Kon-Tiki did in the middle of this
century.

Canoes made of hollowed-out
tree trunks were the next step
from the raft of tree trunks.
The boat was hollowed out with
simple tools or burned out by fire.
Dug-out canoes are still used
all over the world.

Coracle

Kayak

Canoe

Boats and canoes of watertight material stretched over a frame of wood, cane, or bone are found in many lands.

The coracle is almost round. The Eskimo sealskin kayak is slim and pointed. The Indian canoe of North America is long with curving ends.

Boats of planks were built as soon as a way of sealing the cracks between the planks was found.

At first moss was hammered into the seams. Later, tarred cord was used.

Boats built in this way were big
enough to carry many men, and
strong enough to ride heavy seas.
Men began to row farther and
farther from home.

In their longships the Vikings
crossed the seas to Greenland,
Iceland, and even America.

They rowed south to Mediterranean lands, as far as Arabia.
In their long, open boats they often had only a rough tent for shelter. Shields could be fixed along the sides, for the Vikings wanted to conquer as well as to discover new lands.

When the wind was behind them
a mast and sail could be raised
to give more speed and to aid
the rowers.

Long before the Vikings, ship-builders had been busy in the Mediterranean. For thousands of years boats and ships had traveled up and down the Nile and along the seacoast. They were low and broad, with several rowers at each side.

The small fleet of Queen Hatshepsut
of ancient Egypt made an expedition
to the land of Punt, returning with
rich cargoes of ivory, ebony, and
spices, and animals of all kinds.

The Phoenicians were great seamen and traders. Following the coasts, they came to Spain and to Britain. It is said that they may have sailed right around Africa, from the Red Sea to the Mediterranean.

Phoenician bireme

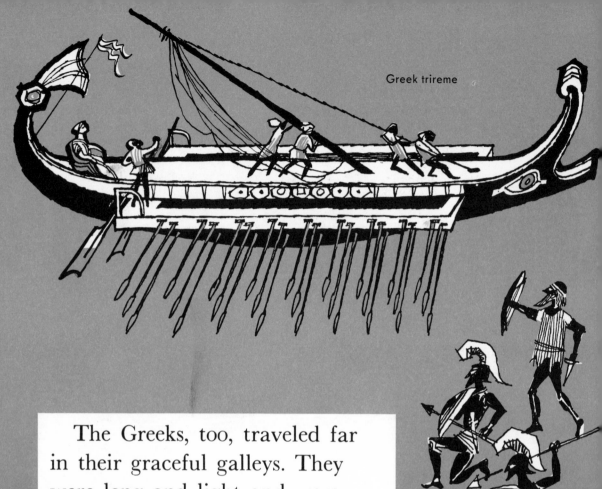

Greek trireme

The Greeks, too, traveled far in their graceful galleys. They were long and light and were steered by two rudder oars. The swift warships often had several banks of oars.

The Greek merchant ships were shorter and broader than the war galleys and were called *round* ships.

Travel by sea was not easy, safe,
or comfortable. Few people made
long sea journeys for pleasure.

Greek sailors often would make
a sacrifice to Poseidon the sea-god
before a voyage, in the hope of fair
weather.

It was a long time before
cabins were built aboard sea-
going ships; and these were for
special people only. The crew
had no cabins.

Roman
merchant ship

Men put to sea or followed the
rivers to trade or to discover
new lands.

The Greeks and Romans found a
way from the Red Sea to India
and China.

Greek
trading vessel

Sometimes men sailed to make
war, or to go on pilgrimages.
The Crusaders voyaged to the
Holy Land for both reasons,
taking their horses with them.

Sails became more important,
until oars were no longer used
to move ships through the water.
A rudder replaced the steering
oar.

Henry V's *Grâce Dieu*

Ships often had more than one mast. Henry V of England had a two-masted ship, in which he sailed to France to war. Henry VIII's *Great Harry* had four masts.

Henry VIII's Great Harry

Under sail the great voyages
of discovery were made.

Prince Henry of Portugal,
called *the Navigator*, sent out
his sea captains to find a new
way to the East.

Columbus' *Santa Maria*

Soon Spanish and Portuguese galleons sailed the seas to new lands to the East and West.

Magellan found a way around South America into the Pacific Ocean. He was the first man to sail around the world.

Magellan's *Victoria*

RETURN TO
CAMPBELL UNION SCHOOL
DISTRICT LIBRARY

Discard

Captain Francis Drake was the next to do it. Of his fleet of five ships only his own ship the *Golden Hind* returned to England.

Soon there were great fleets of merchant ships sailing between the East and West Indies and Europe.

Captain James Cook spent many years sailing and exploring the Pacific. He found the way to keep his seamen healthy and comfortable. He took limes, oranges, and lemons to eat and he made his men keep themselves and the ship clean.

Cook's *Endeavour*
1768

In the seventeenth century ships'
hulls were richly carved and
painted.

In the eighteenth century the
hulls were simpler. The only
ornaments were figureheads and
decorations on the stern.

A steering wheel was used
to move the big rudder.

Sovereign of the Seas
1637

Ariel, Taeping and Serica

Sailing ships became faster
than ever when copper was fitted
over the wooden hull below the
waterline.

The graceful clipper ships,
carrying tea, wool, and grain,
sped around the world. They often
raced each other.

In 1866 *Ariel*, *Serica* and *Taeping* raced sixteen thousand miles from Foochow in China to the Thames in England.

Eighteen years before, Captain Kettle had sailed the Chinese junk *Keying* from China to the Thames.

Keying

31

In the nineteenth century many
people moved from Europe to
America and Australia. They had
unhealthy and uncomfortable
journeys. There were no proper
cabins, and they had to take
their own food with them for the
voyage.

Small steamship, about 1800

Travel by sea was far pleasanter with the coming of the ocean liners, built of iron and driven by steam.

Small steamships had been used for short journeys for several years before a steamship crossed the Atlantic.

Rattler 1845

The packet-steamer *Savannah* steamed from America to Ireland in 1819. The early steamships still had masts and sails, to add extra speed.

Savannah

Alecto 1845

Later, a tug-of-war at sea between the warships H.M.S. *Rattler* and H.M.S. *Alecto* proved that a screw propeller was far stronger than a paddle wheel. The *Rattler* won.

Brunel's *Great Eastern* used paddle wheels as well as a screw propeller.

Great Eastern 1858

MAURETANIA

When the small ship *Turbinia*, driven by strong new engines called *turbines*, raced in the English Channel in 1897, none of the other fast ships could catch her.

Soon great ships of steel were using turbines.

TURBINIA

TURBINIA

Liner *United States*

The Cunard liner *Mauretania*, driven by turbines, won the Blue Riband of the Atlantic for being the fastest ship on the Atlantic run.

Now large, swift liners carry passengers and cargoes safely and regularly across the Atlantic.

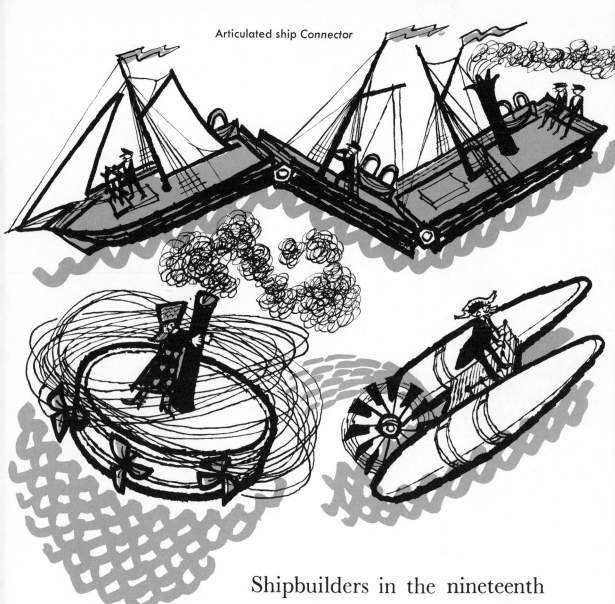

Articulated ship Connector

Shipbuilders in the nineteenth century had many strange ideas about the shape of ships in the future; but few of them worked.

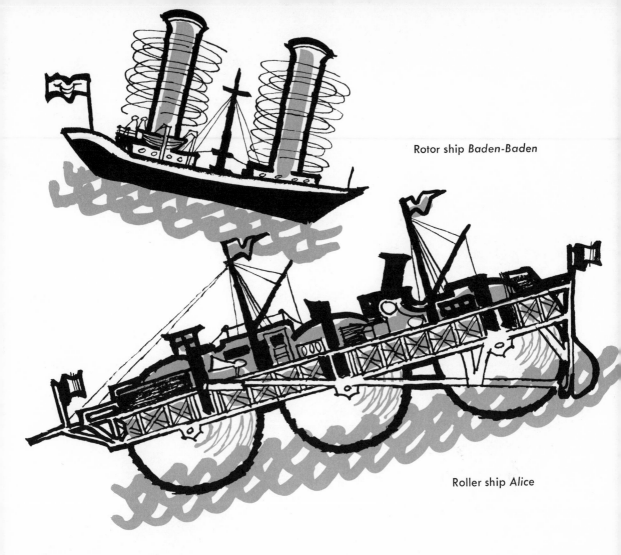

Rotor ship *Baden-Baden*

Roller ship *Alice*

No ship, however it was driven
or whatever its shape, could
ever have got very far without
instruments to find the way.

Early sailors had few
instruments and so rarely left
sight of land. They used the sun
and stars to steer by.

Over the years instruments
were devised. Without them
new lands may never
have been found
or charted.

16th-century astrolabe

Joshua Slocum could not have sailed around the world on his own without an up-to-date compass. It helped him sail in the right direction. To work out his position at sea he also needed a sextant and a chronometer, which is an accurate timepiece.

In 1895 Captain Slocum set out in Spray

Captain Joshua Slocum

Compass

Sextant

Chronometer

41

Now there are many thousands
of ships at sea, big and small.
All depend on safe ports and
harbors. They rely on lights,
tugs, and pilots to guide them
into safe waters.

Should there be a wreck, the
lifeboats are always alert to
bring help.

Big ships sometimes can go a
long way inland up large rivers.
But often only small boats, tugs,
and barges can continue upstream
and along the canals which criss-
cross many countries.

Rivers are important highways
the world over. The canal net-
works which link big rivers and
towns are always busy.

Men also have to cross rivers
as well as travel up and down
them, and ferryboats go to and
fro across almost every big
river.

Hovercraft

There always will be new
ideas for travel by water.
Submarines now glide silently
underwater.

Hydroplane

Hovercraft glide across the
surface.

Men skate over the water at
high speed in hydroplanes and on
water skis and scooters, or
wobble along on boat-shoes.

But the old ideas, which have
been in use for centuries, remain.
The rivers and oceans have been
explored, but men still go about
in boats.